THE MYTH

TITLED

"UNEMPLOYMENT"

GOD'SWILL C OLEMGBE

Copyright © 2015 Olemgbe God'swill C
All rights reserved.
ISBN-10: 1511841133
ISBN-13: 978- 1511841139

DEDICATION

I thankfully dedicate this book to God Almighty; the owner of the whole universe, who from his abundance has endured the Earth with so much opportunity for all mankind.

CONTENTS

	Acknowledgments	i
	Preface	iii
1	Unemployment is Abuse	1
2	Resources on earth	10
3	Why you will remain Unemployed	19
4	Opportunities for no cost	30
5	Your Hobby is Your Gateway	38
6	Conclusion	42
7	About the Author	45

ACKNOWLEDGMENTS

The Myth Titled Unemployment emerged from a very exceptional moment. Occupied with so many things to do and can't do them because of been tied up at some other place; even as a student. Yet news in the air fill men's ears with unemployment statistics; its more than a tale.
This is my opinion and in no wise conclusive!
My heart felt gratitude goes to all those that has taught me both in pains and excitement. They made me know exactly what it takes to succeed and more importantly, has empowered me to speak.
And my college that has allowed me learn from my journey through university; wishing to be out of school and trying to compensate for years unaccounted for. It's an experience, I will remain ever thankful for: out of the mess indeed came this fine gold.

PREFACE

This book is about unemployment as a myth; in relation to the accidental state of believe held by citizens of the present Millennia: the most advance of all generation human generation.

As an issue of principal concern, it has been encouraged by the general public, media, government, research and policies; even though it seems a though it makes so much sense. What has been done about it?

I believe that if this will be taken up as a cooperate responsibility by all the respective stakeholders; more positive objective will be achieved. Not ignoring the fact the human policies and advancement are designed to treat effects, and not effect change; they lag behind human evolution in all case.

I am mandated to reason, that this book is making sufficiently clear; what is meant here by the term, "the unemployed" as relating to the complexities of people from different walks of life. I have given such setting that should resound in men's heart, the integral understand behind the goal of life, and well developed attributes of a life worth living. And so far as I could, describe the term unemployment as unreal and mythical.

There are two ways nature have made available for you to be gainfully employed. The first is for you to look at for what people do or need and convert that into your opportunity. The second is to take what your love doing; nature's personal gift to you, your talent and grow your money tree. Follow through, as we take an in-depth look into these opportunities.

1

UNEMPLOYMENT IS ABUSE

A search of all the synonyms of the term unemployment has nothing positive to say; it makes it obvious. Been defined as nothing but wanton joblessness and non-productivity; yet, this term has found so much peace and approval with men.

We see creature and the natural environment responding to duty call every day. The sun resumes to its only job; to give light and heat. The moon does same, the wind is at its own; hey, every natural content is at it: employed and doing exactly what it knows how to do best.

If we all believe nature abhors no vacuum and indeed nature despises non productivity; could it then be true that someone somewhere has nothing to do, but sit and wander for as long as 6 months and above? Human vacuity!

> *"The cool thing about unemployment is every day is Saturday."*
> *Jarod*

Let's talk about you for a moment. If you do everything for a purpose, go to college to get a degree, get a job to pay your bills, marry because of love and companionship or whatever, and exercise to keep fit. Wouldn't it be right then to say emphatically that the creator of life must have created you or perhaps allowed your existence for a purpose. It may not mean much to us you, but I belong to the school of thought that believes in the existence of a supernatural being, behind creation.

The natural course of things is towards disorderliness; so to have achieved the orderliness we have in the universe today, a supreme being is obviously at work. The universe is not a happenstance, and if not a happenstance, then the creator must have created everything to fulfil a purpose. The failure of man to live without engaging with his responsibility on earth, is abuse of opportunity.

What's unemployment saying...

Unemployment quietly states that there are some certain group of persons that are currently unproductive as far as the economy of the earth is concern. These individuals are only relevant as consumers. They constitute an increase to the number of poverty head count, uses up earth natural resources and play no significant role to the greater wellbeing of planet earth. What a sorry state to be!

It also tells us that such people account for a larger part of most developing nations.; having over 50% of their population living below standard poverty line. To complicate issues, they are confortable been addressed as unemployed.

> *The failure of man to live without engaging with his responsibility on earth is abuse of opportunity.*

The purpose of man

When you have a garden; what do you do to the garden? If you're responsible enough to have owned a garden, you will cultivate the garden and ensure everything is in it right place.

Let's employ your imagination. Can you see man placed in a big garden called planet earth for a purpose, to cultivate for the earth, to ensure the safety and continuous existence of the earth: called sustainability; to provide service, to enjoy the resources and after a hard time labour, retire in peace. Good job.

"People keep asking what I do for a living and I keep saying that I don't believe in making a living. That it's a concept that has been twisted. I tell them I believe in making a life, and money is a distracting object if there's anything left at the end of the day; and I just want to go on well. Make it through the day. So I smile and raise my glass and they laugh and take my hand, saying "here's to the youth", pointing at me.

And I might just be young and naïve for I still believe in the freedom of choice of how to spend your life. So they toast to the youth, who still think she's free, and that's all fine by me." — *Charlotte Eriksson*

The Growing population on earth

The population of the earth is currently rated at over 7 billion people and it still on the increase daily. Economics tells us that the needs of man are insatiable, and if this holds true; then the demand of service by men will never be saturated.

Men will never stop buying; they will not stop travelling, feeding, clothing, marrying and going on vacation. This simply means, man will continue to be in need of one service, goods or the other they cannot provide for themselves. This must be provided by a third party. That is an employment opportunity for someone.

Currently, no country or continent is independent and saturated with every resource it needs, nor will any be tomorrow. Mechanization was thought to be the climax of science; today, is but a past, as we are thousand times faster than the days before. Demands keep emerging, and opportunity is its faithful companion for the visionary few on earth.

What am I trying to say? The more people on earth keep going through civilization, population keeps increasing, and the distribution of resources continues to increase; this will make more opportunity and resultantly more money available for everyone.

Imagine Seven (7) billion unique needs to be provided; only the visionary can see the opportunity. Unemployment is not real, but a myth. A problem created and serviced by men. There is someone somewhere whose needs are not met, who has the money to pay and is in need of a service you can offer.

2

RESOURCES ON EARTH

We live in the midst of enumerable amount of wealth that the human mind cannot phantom. No matter how much the richest people on earth today have gathered in their possession, they do not possess 1% of the resources on earth. It therefore means, there's enough of everything to make everyone absolutely rich and enjoy an above average lifestyle. The challenge is that most young people have an deep-seated scarcity mentality; that needs to be expunged.

The entire universe, including the earth we live in, uses only small portion of the sun's energy; it does not operate or live by a scarcity mentality. It is a world of abundance. If nature knows its skirted with so much abundance and operates with such decorum; how then are men ravaged by scarcity of responsibility and opportunity to be gainfully employed?

Something happened somewhere. Follow

me, as we look at some resources at your disposal for maximum utilization.

AIR

There is gas everywhere you can think about. In it are mixtures that are of economic value, including oxygen, the very gas that keeps us going. It sustains the whole cycle of living things and also provides job for millions of persons working in the gas sector. Most importantly, the potentials of the gas sector are still untapped

> *The challenge is that most young people have an deep-seated scarcity mentality; that needs to be expunged.*

and its full potential is yet unknown.

WATER

I am certain you cannot do without water for one day. The water you see as common, perhaps just drink callously, is making things happen, and above all it is sustaining life at one level and providing job at another level. Millions are living on it and many are yet to live on it. It's the one important solution on the earth of immense value and universal acceptance.

EARTH

The earth is the store house of minerals and all manner of precious metals. It is home to plants and animals, doing job at that level. At another level, is providing job opportunity to billions of persons on earth. I am of the opinion that all the earth hold have not been discovered and cannot be exhausted no matter what science thinks about depletion. One of it minerals may be used up, but not all its minerals. The earth has enough to gainfully employ you.

YOU

You're a product of all and live on all. That makes you more powerful and more resourceful. Everything not natural that exists in your cycle of life is the work of human imagination and creativity: the display of peak intellectual capacity of a genius being. A class you belong. You are still untapped; you're loaded with so much potential, waiting to be put to work. "What is the good of being a genius if you cannot use it as an excuse for being unemployed?" ~Gerald Barzan

> *You are still untapped; you're loaded with so much potential, waiting to be put to work.*

History has shown how man unravelled opportunity available for employment on the human body. The finger nails were just nails until someone somewhere thought they could be better taken care of for a pay, today millions of persons are gainfully employed doing manicure and pedicure. Same applies to the hair and other parts of the human body. Permit me to say that all the economy of the earth is centred about meeting the needs of man, and those are not satiable.

Another amazing thing about the world is that all it resources are at every man's disposal for free. What you make out of them is strictly your own. If you're in a country like mine, some people package and sell water for business, they don't pay for the water, but people pay to get the water from them. Some go on gold search, and lots more to be done.

There is so much out there for free, find it and the world will pay you the fee.

Learn how to put the resources to achieve your desired goal. Learn how to pull it together to meet a need, discover something new and set a pace for another generation. There is so much yet undiscovered in the midst of earth, water and air. Get into the business of creativity, and you will know no bounds,

The needs of man are not satiable and can never be satiable. There are needs to be met in your neighbourhood, the underdeveloped and less developed economies; all are in need of human essential services to make life on earth full and enjoyable: get involved and engage now!

3

WHY YOU WILL REMAIN UNEMPLOYED

Having seen the aura of opportunity that exist all around you and in you, waiting to gainfully employ you and others around you; there are also very obvious reason why perhaps you have remain unemployed and will remain unemployed even amidst these wealth if not addressed.

Of this are three obvious reasons that have kept the world under the bondage of unemployment. As a man thinket in his heart so is he says the great teacher, the world thinks unemployment and are ravished by its syndrome even though it just a myth. So "don't stop searching until you find creative and gainful Unemployment" Dean Cavanagh.

> *An unemployed generation is a wasted generation, "unfortunately, very few governments think about youth unemployment when they are drawing up their national plans" Kofi Annan.*

KNOWLEDGE

Knowledge is a principal thing. Nothing empowers like knowledge and there is no height of bondage and slavery than ignorance. Ignorance of purpose and the availability of life without a purpose have caused many undelivered dream to end in the grave. Many giant a vision has passed over the earth without seeing the light of day, because the carriers of such never knew the earth await for their manifestation, while the wandered it surface looking for what was inside them. "unemployment is a weapon of mass destruction" Dennis Kucinich.

Every job opportunity out there was made

or polished by man, none came as it is today by nature; nature does not employ, men employ and until men in every generation provide the platform, the generation will remain unemployed. *An unemployed generation is a wasted generation, "unfortunately, very few governments think about youth unemployment when they are drawing up their national plans" Kofi Annan.*

BUREAUCRACY

Bureaucracy is man's way of obeying the law of evolution. "Just as a CEO could care less about pay equity, the university administrator is unconcerned with how many of her program graduates, secure employment of any particular quality" Joseph Ohler, Jr. It keys to the fact that the best fit enjoys the highest and best of advantages that cannot absolve all the graduates. However, this do not define you, because every man is more powerful than can be defined by human bureaucratic measures. Such limitations have been accepted by many and have caused many a talents and destiny to be wasted.

> *Bureaucracy is man's way of obeying the law of evolution:*

Wake, break the bar and be on the move. We will take a look at four of these nasty human activities below:

☐ QUALIFICATION

All the opportunities advertised are listing so long a list of qualification as the criteria to apply; not a guarantee even after meeting all that. They are trying to say, if you don't have this, you don't belong here; hey, get on the go, find where you belong or go get what it takes to belong there. Just the paper though.

☐ EXPERIENCE

Years of experience principally tells the young man in his strength, we don't need your strength, we need experience. We need people that know what they are doing, people that have put their capacity to test and delivered expected outcomes. You don't have that and we don't have space for novice entrepreneurs like you. Get a life dude, by giving the real you a life experience.

☐ CITIZENSHIP

Some work positions are reserved for particular persons of a given citizenship; or perhaps you are living in a foreign land. Don't wait and wastes, the earth is yet to truly become a global village, get up and go where you're celebrated and not tolerated; Your home land! After all, there's no place like home says an old adage.

☐ CONNECTION

If you are from a country like mine, then

you must know someone that knows someone to get the job. It's called on the job recommendation or reference. Well, I bet you know someone; and that is the you that knows you, and can give you the job you need. Man know thyself is a popular saying; they key to living they very life you are made to live.

> *Don't wait and wastes, the earth is yet to truly become a global village, get up and go where you're celebrated and not tolerated.*

YOU

The third category of factor that has kept man unemployed from ages and has the potential to keep you and generation's unborn unemployed for life is the You in you. There is nothing as powerful as you and nothing can stop you except that which you allow. We cannot review all factors here and how to deal with them, but the great book speaks about poverty abiding in the house of he who goes after sleep and slumber. Laziness will keep you unemployed, so is resentment and

> *You are a generational factor in ending employment and you have stopped men from been gain fully employed today and in the future.*

irresponsibility.

The job you create today will remove you from the unemployment list and perhaps provide job for a thousand others in the coming generation. "Working hard is a fool's anthem, getting others to work for you is the motto for every successful man" Michael Bassey Johnson.

Your failure to deliver the job you carry leaves future generation of men to be born into the cycle of unemployment, because you failed to create the needed job. You are a generational factor in ending employment and you have stopped men from been gain fully employed today and in the future.

"You look at the jobless as a huge pile of scrap and you're looking for what can be recycled. That's good. That's your job. But what you don't realise is that this pile of scrap itself serves a purpose. I need my zeros, Eric. They put fear in people; fear of crime and terrorism. They are a stark reminder to the stakeholders that what they despise today, they may end up joining tomorrow. It keeps them obedient. Remember that!"

Mark Cantrell, Citizen Zero

4
OPPORTUNITIES FOR NO COST

Nature has provided equal opportunity for everyone to succeed, no matter what dispensation you were born. All men are endowed naturally with inherent talent and ability to survive. "What is required as we travel towards full unemployment is not new legislation, but a gradual change of mental attitude and a shift in values. As our taste for idling grows, we will refuse to work for old-fashioned bosses who demand a five-day, 40-hour, nine-to-five type week, or worse" Tom Hodgkinson.

Let's look at some things you can do for no cost today; others are gainfully employed this way and you are no exception. If one can, then all can!

> *Anyone has an opportunity in the internet. Just anyone!*

INTERNET

This is a world of its own, presenting very unique and diversified opportunity for all. If you choose to live on earth today and live outside the internet: you are of all historic men most archaic. Whatever you may think about doing today that has no business with the internet, is no business at all. It has become the central hub of all man's activity. The opportunities are obvious. They under listed services are available on the internet for no fee; they include blogging, information marketing, affiliate marketing and sales agent, sell creative products of arts online, editing jobs, freelancer writing, virtual assistant, online

> *Your ideas cost no money and you don't need to be employed to have useful ideas.*

consulting and design among others.

The amazing thing about the internet is that it requires just basic typing and editing skills, both males and females are getting empowered by having access to the internet. Anyone, I repeat, anyone has an opportunity in the internet. Just anyone!

IDEA

Your ideas cost no money and you don't need to be employed to have useful ideas. Been devoid of a job does not mean you don't have a brain. People sell ideas to make a living. People have excellent ideas about how existing companies can do better, sell it to them and get paid; they move on to the next one and you keep helping enterprise improve their products and services. You must not implement all your ideas, someone may have to run with, sell it and make your living, after all, there's so much more where the initial one came from; your thinking box.

COMPETITION

There are lots and lots of competition going on every day, you could join or organize one. Invite participant's, gets sponsorship/ Someone started the Olympic, and the next big thing to happen is in you.

WRITING AND CREATIVE ARTS

Everyone who went through high school

can write, whatever it is, you've got something special and unique to you to tell the world, just write it or do the art work; we want to see it. Don't die with that entire event going on in your head. Put it down, enter writing competitions, review books, and make a living. Without taking the pain to put this down, you might never see it, I do not how far away we are apart, but sure, if my books can get to you; so can yours. Get creative with your hands today.

> *The world never stops buying, when you learn to never stop selling and that makes you a living.*

SPORT

Sport is a multibillion dollar industry. You play sports yet it's just for fitness but you spend your most precious hours of the morning doing it, several times a week. People are living a number one lifestyle on sports, get out there and get paid for what you do. Apply for the local club listings, go for the audition, show what you got and get paid for it.

SALES

No mater your qualification, sales is the world number one economy equalizer. It's the best paying non-professional job, and you know what; you need no qualification and no money to get on the sales job. The world never stops buying, when you learn to never stop selling and that makes you a living. Remember it must not be your stuff before it can be sold, all you need do is find something someone needs and offer to provide, earn the commission and make your living. After all, a lot of company's out there are looking for interested persons to recruit into direct sale; the sales force of next generation sales.

5

YOUR HOBBY
IS YOUR GATEWAY

So far we've been trying to explain how you can get employed by what people do; a simple business philosophy also practiced by Warren Buffet who said "what I love doing should be my hobby, what the world does should be my business". However, beyond this, is another unique opportunity that nature has giving you, a talent that allows you to be branded; to be you and just you.

It is your door way to providing service to humanity while having fun with life; an endowment that comes out of your innate strength. Not limited by all the human induced factors that further strengthens unemployment. Above all, it allows you an opportunity to be the best. Remember, nature has a way of letting the best access the best it has to offer. It is your platform to accessing

> *Find your place before you get there.*

the best the earth can offer.

Look deep inside you, there's something you love doing, something you do for pleasure, for the peace of mind it gives you and begin to sharpen it edges. Show it out, and put it up for display because somewhere out there, some dude is making a living from your hobby.

YOUR TALENT: NOT FOR PLAY BUT FOR PAY

Nobody goes to college, or farm for the fun of it only; everyone expects a pay day. By putting your talents to efficient use, and adequately given to the service of humanity, will offer you the highest pay and satisfaction in life.

I heard this story about talents narrated in a meeting I attended while in the university and wish I could credit properly. Talents says I am a gift, give me to self, and I will make you happy, give me to friends and loved ones, I will add to your treasures, give me to the world and I will multiply your treasures and bring the world to you. A simple illustration of what given your talent out can do to your life.

6
CONCLUSION

The great book says there's work, but only in the grave. Unemployment is valid therefore only in the grave, but even the cemetery is someone else's work place. Find your place before you get there.

When men need money; they go to the banks, when they need land; they to the land department, when they need security; they go to the security agencies, when they need real human capital, where do they go to? There is employment; the scarce commodity is essential and certified human capital.

Develop yourself today to become an employer of labour, and employment will look for you.

> *There is employment; the scarce commodity is essential and certified human capital.*

"Let's all roll up our sleeves and get back to work. Or let's create jobs where other people roll up other people's sleeves, so these other people can get to work helping other people get to work" Jarod Kintz.

See you on the other side and congratulations for taking the bold step to get to the end.

Get my next book, "Human Capital: A Universal Scarcity"

To your success

Olemgbe God'swill C

ABOUT THE AUTHOR

Olemgbe God'swill C, a Medical Student with the College of Health Sciences University of Abuja, is a dynamic and entertaining speaker; actively dedicated to the training and development of young minds.

He is the Northern Zonal Representative of Anglican Student Fellowship, and an Associate Fellow of the Royal Commonwealth Commission.

Olemgbe, an award winner of Several Writing Competitions, is a frequent guest speaker nationally at conferences and has authored four other brief titles.

If you have any questions about Olemgbe God'swill events and programs, or want to have him in any event, please email: info@nisce.com.ng or call +2348055954094.

www.ingramcontent.com/pod-product-compliance
Lightning Source LLC
Chambersburg PA
CBHW021040180526
45163CB00005B/2216